Warne's Transport Library

Trucks of the Sixties and Seventies

compiled by Nick Baldwin

FREDERICK WARNE

Published by Frederick Warne (Publishers) Ltd London 1980

Also in Warne's Transport Library

Farm Tractors by Nick Baldwin
English Horse Drawn Vehicles by David Parry
French Cars 1920–25 by Pierre Dumont
Blue Blood by Serge Bellu
The GMC—a Universal Truck by J-M Boniface and J-G Jeudy

ISBN 0 7232 2364 5

Filmset and printed in Great Britain by
BAS Printers Limited, Over Wallop, Hampshire
1286.879

CONTENTS

INTRODUCTION

The past twenty years have seen more changes in trucks and trucking than in possibly the whole of their previous existence. Trucks have become larger and more powerful than ever before and yet technological progress has made them far safer, quieter and more economical. During the sixties and seventies we have seen the almost universal adoption of tilt cabs to improve engine accessibility, the widespread use of turbochargers to increase power, more sophisticated transmissions, and tremendous improvements in driver environment. Not all truck firms have been able to keep up with these changes, and, as will be seen on the following pages, several have been swallowed up or defeated.

Manufacturers have been included under country headings, and the order of these is based on their relative output of trucks above 6 tons gross in the mid seventies. The only one that might be out of order is the USSR, which is grouped with all the Eastern European countries. Together they probably make more trucks than any other country, but they do not release figures of a kind which can be directly compared.

It is obviously impossible to do full justice to all the types of truck that have been available in the past twenty years in the following pages — indeed any one sizeable manufacturer will have made more different types than there are photos in this book — so what I have attempted to do is to include a good cross-section of years and makes to help show the styling and technical changes that have taken place.

I have been greatly helped in my choice of photographs by Elliott Kahn, Nick Georgano, Arthur Ingram, Charles Bernoski, John Aldridge and my colleagues at Marshall, Harris & Baldwin Ltd.

If you feel that the book is unfairly biased towards the sixties I can only state in my defence that I enjoyed looking back more than describing vehicles that are familiar on the road today, and in any event, these are described in the current edition of *The Observer's Book of Commercial Vehicles*, which makes a useful companion volume to this book.

Nearly all the terms used in the following pages are well known to 'trucking types' and need no explanation though I should perhaps point out that gvw is gross vehicle weight (rigid vehicle), gcw — gross combined weight (usually artic) and gtw — gross train weight (truck and laden trailer(s)). Gas or gasoline is of course the American word for petrol and cab-over, conventional, hood and fender are respectively forward control, normal control, bonnet and wing in Britain.

NICK BALDWIN, September 1979

USA

Though small numbers of the heavy US trucks had been diesel powered since the mid thirties, medium trucks were slow in adopting diesel until the late fifties and lighter trucks did so even later. In 1956 less than 2 per cent of trucks in America were diesel powered and this had risen to 3.5 per cent in 1962. This apparent lethargy was explained to a great extent by America's supply of cheap petrol.

In the early years of mass conversion to diesel in the sixties, Perkins were supplying over 25,000 engines a year from Britain (mainly to White, Dodge and International) and they ultimately bought the Hercules engine factory from White to increase this business. Ford also imported diesels from their British factories. However, General Motors' Detroit division and Cummins soon moved into the smaller horsepower diesel market, and were later joined by Caterpillar.

During the past twenty years there has been a considerable reduction in the number of American makers of commercial vehicles, while output has risen. The vast difference in size between the specialist heavy vehicle makers and the mass producers in the early sixties is shown by these approximate 1962 figures for medium and heavy truck production. Of all these firms the one with the highest production of diesel engined trucks in 1962 was Mack with 11,000 units.

Autocar	1,450	FWD	1,000	Kenworth	1,500
Brockway	1,300	Ford	92,400	Mack	14,000
Chevrolet	76,900	Freightliner	2,000	Reo	7,500
Diamond T	2,100	GMC	40,800	Studebaker	7,400
Dodge	20,100	International	75,000	White	13,300

America was the first country to experiment with gas turbines in trucks: turbine-powered American La France and Kenworth in the early sixties, followed by pre-production models from Ford, GMC, International and others from the mid sixties. Throughout the sixties and seventies cab-over (forward control) trucks had tilt cabs — an American development of the fifties.

Diamond-Reo

Diamond-Reo was a new name in trucks that came about in 1967 with the combination of the old-established Diamond T and Reo firms. Both had belonged to the White Motor Company since the late fifties and had therefore been stablemates of Autocar.

In 1971 Diamond-Reo became an independent company but went out of business four years later. Diamond-Reo designs were sold to several firms including Osterlund of Camp Hill, who also purchased the Diamond-Reo name for the designs they put into production.

Diamond T's fibreglass tilt cab, shown in 1960. Similar styling was used by Reo and International. The 634CG model shown had a 6-cylinder Reo 331 cu.in 170bhp (185bhp optional) gasoline engine and choice of 5- or 8-speed gearbox.

Introduced in 1959, the Diamond T 931 CN was available with various Cummins diesels of up to 280bhp. The 50in deep tilt cab was of aluminium and fibreglass and was the forerunner of the Royale cab. Gtw was 76,800lbs.

Reo conventional (normal control) models looked similar to some of the conventional Diamond T's but with smaller windscreens. This is a 1964 E456 with 3 driven rear axles and single tyres all round, giving maximum traction and weight distribution with minimum tyre scrub and transfer of site slurry. Reo Gold Crown gasoline engines and Cummins diesels of up to 250bhp were available.

Following the separation of Diamond-Reo and White, this is a 1973 Royale tractive unit with Detroit diesel engine. Even at this late stage gasoline and LPG engines were available.

Dodge

As the truck-producing arm of the Chrysler Corporation, Dodge attempted to offer a full range of light to heavy trucks in the sixties to compete with GMC and Ford. However, sales of the heavier models were slow and in the mid seventies they concentrated their efforts on the 30,000lb gvw market and below.

Chrysler of course also owned Dodge trucks in Britain until 1978, when this division was acquired by Peugeot-Citroën, who at the same time bought Dodge/Barreiros in Spain, which had been a Chrysler subsidiary since 1970. Dodges produced for certain export territories have been marketed under the names Fargo and De Soto.

Dodge's heavy truck range used this style of cab through to 1974 and 228bhp V-8 gas engines or various Cummins diesels to 195bhp. Thermostatic radiator shutters were standard and fenders (wings) hinged outwards to aid engine accessibility. Gcw was up to 55,000lbs. A 700 series example is shown here as seen at work in 1970.

Also available with Dodge lettering was this 1971 Fargo heavy duty model with L Series aluminium tilt cab and 200 to 335bhp Cummins or Detroit diesels. Cab depth was only 49in BBC (bumper to back of cab) or 79in with the sleeper cab.

New for the 1973 season were the D500, D600 and D800 with this revised styling, and gvw ranging from 14,800 to 29,750lbs. These were available with pre-select gearboxes. Various petrol engine options were available. In the later seventies Dodge concentrated on lighter trucks.

Ford

Ever since Ford had introduced their C range in 1957 as the cheapest cab-over tilt-cab trucks in America, they gained an increasing share of the truck market. Their heaviest H models were replaced in mid 1966 by the W, which is still produced in their premium range. The conventional L (Louisville) range of late 1969 onwards remained in production of course at the end of the seventies, as did the C after some 22 years. The heavy models use Caterpillar, Cummins and Detroit diesels.

The heaviest Fords in 1963 were the N-Series and this 6 x 4 tractor has a choice of Cummins in-line 6-cylinder diesels of up to 250bhp.

New in 1966 was the W range with Cummins, Detroit and Caterpillar diesels of 195 to 335bhp. They could have 10-ton capacity single rear axles or 15-ton tandems. Discontinued 1978.

An H-Series tilt-cab model of 1962. The 2-axle version was for gcw of up to 76,800lbs and could have V-8 gasoline or choice of Cummins diesels up to 220bhp.

Suitable for a gvw of around 50,000lbs, this C-Series tandem of 1972 had choice of V-8 diesel and 6-cylinder and V-8 gas engines. Its basic cab design first appeared in 1957 and continued throughout the sixties and seventies.

1973 F750 had 361cu.in or 391cu.in Ford V-8 gas engines and a gvw of 27,500lbs. This has the more luxuriously trimmed Custom cab, as shown by the chrome grille.

The L-Line of trucks and tractors appeared in time for the 1970 model season and have been produced all through the decade. They have Ford gas or diesel engines plus the option of Cummins or Detroit diesels. The tandem example shown, of the mid seventies, is for gtw of up to 80,000lbs.

General Motors

Though both part of General Motors, GMC and Chevrolet trucks are marketed separately. GMC makes the heavy and many of the medium sized trucks for both names, while all the lightweight GM units are Chevrolet built. GM owns the makers of Detroit diesels. GMC itself has manufactured diesel engines, but these have not been in production since 1975.

Detroit diesels are unusual in that they operate on the 2-stroke principle which is claimed to benefit fuel consumption and save weight. As well as using diesels, GMC had the most powerful gas truck engine in use in the early sixties, a V-12 of 275bhp output and they were also early experimenters with gas turbine trucks in 1965.

GMC trucks are affectionately known as Jimmies in the States, while Chevrolets are of course Chevies.

9

Here we see a 1967 Series 70 Chevrolet, passing through an electronic load height senser. It had choice of 210 or 225bhp V-6 gas engines or Detroit diesels. When equipped with tandem axles a gtw of up to 65,000lbs was permitted.

A typical example of GMC's famous high tilt cab (48in BBC) range shown at work on the Chrysler Expressway in Detroit in 1963. It has a Detroit V-8 290bhp diesel engine, and in this tractor/trailer combination it could handle 57½-ton loads of earth.

A Chevrolet N50 of 1965 with 118bhp V-6 gas engine. It had a tilt cab and was primarily for local distribution. A similar cab was used on GMC's L range.

With extras to suit heavy duty 'West Coast' operating conditions in arduous highway haulage and logging, this is a 1966 GMC. The 114in BBC cab was based on their standard 92in version but given a long fibreglass hood (bonnet) and fenders (wings) that hinged forwards for access. This gave uncluttered room for V-6 and V-8 Detroit diesels, the largest 303bhp engine allowing a gvw of 53,000lbs and a combination weight far higher.

The heaviest line haul models were replaced in the late sixties by the GMC Astro 95. This is a 1969 example with aluminium tilt cab and choice of engines up to 318bhp.

Broadly similar to the Astro 95 was Chevrolet's Titan 90, which like the Astro had an option of either Detroit or Cummins power. Over 50 transmission options were available and though the models were joined by a conventional (normal control) General in '76 they are still General Motors' most popular heavy models.

New Fleetstar A models in 1968 consisted of these conventional 4- and 6-wheelers with 6-cylinder and V-8 petrol engines and V-8 diesels for up to 54,000lbs gvw and up to 65,000lbs gtw. The two optional hood (bonnet) styles are shown, butterfly on the left and one-piece fibreglass on the right.

Based on the contemporary Transtar 230 to 335bhp line haul unit, this is a 1968 prototype gas turbine truck. It had a Solar (an International Harvester Co. subsidiary) 300-plus bhp turbine with what was claimed to be the first stationary integral heat exchanger. The 34,000rpm output was reduced to 4000rpm and fed through a normal 5-speed gearbox. Production was planned for 1970 but technical difficulties and the absence of any clear-cut fuel economy put an end to this.

International

International has enjoyed a unique position among American truck manufacturers in that it makes a very full range of light to heavy vehicles — 'the world's most complete line' as it was called in 1961. It thus competes with everything from Ford to Mack and yet it is neither a car maker nor an expensive premium truck maker.

Unlike its car and truck making competitors, International has its power base in agricultural and construction machinery, and this has meant a useful background of diesel technology. In addition it is able to borrow from European experience through its part share in DAF, and since 1974 its ownership of

11

International's CO line (with Diamond T made cab) of 1960 included 2- and 3-axle rigids and tractive units of 25,000lbs gvw to 65,000lbs gtw. The cab tilted, and engines were International's own Red Diamond gasoline units of 190 to 225bhp. 5- or 8-speed gearboxes, the former with optional torque converter, were offered. Soon afterwards Cummins diesels were also available.

Bearing a striking resemblance to the Bedford TK is this 1964 Loadstar with redesigned CO cab. It used the Perkins 6.354 6-cylinder diesel developing 131bhp and was available as a rigid, or as in this case, as a short-wheelbase tractive unit for urban manoeuvrability.

Developed from the successful heavy-duty Paystar range are these 1978 S-Series models — 2600 on left, then 2500 and 2200. Various Cummins, Detroit, Caterpillar and International engines in the 200 to 350bhp range are available.

Mack

Until diesels became universal in heavy American trucks in the seventies, Mack always outsold the other diesel truck makers, and was unusual in making all its own engines, though proprietary types also became available. Mack's large diesels pioneered the high torque, constant horsepower concept in the sixties, and today these Maxidyne engines are used in most of the larger models, whilst engines built in collaboration with Scania are used in most trucks under 200bhp.

The F-Series forward-control tilt-cab models were launched in 1962 and here is one in slightly unfamiliar guise — a 1966 Mack Western 'West Coast' FL700 model. It used aluminium alloy for chassis, cab, wheels and hubs, and could have engines of 187 to 380bhp, built in Mack's new Californian factory opened in 1966.

Perhaps the most famous of all Macks after their legendary pre-war AC Bulldogs were the B-Series conventionals of the fifties and early sixties. Shown is a 6 × 4 B-42 tipper at work in 1961. It had a 187bhp 6-cylinder Mack Thermodyne diesel.

A recent Mack cab-over is the Cruise-Liner range and shown here is a 1977 rigid six with aluminium and fibreglass tilt cab. A steel or aluminium chassis is optional and Mack, Cummins, Caterpillar or Detroit diesels of 235 to 450bhp are available.

White

White has been a major truck producer throughout the period, but without the financial success of its most comparable rivals, International and Mack. It continues to own Autocar, which it bought in 1953, but it was forced to part with Diamond-Reo and its Hercules engine plant, as well as several other divisions. It has also had exclusive marketing arrangements with the Freightliner Corporation, who now distribute Volvo trucks in America as well as making their own Freightliners.

A contrast in styles, with a 1963 C-series (left) alongside a 1973 U-700. The 11½in offset cab of the U gave better vision for the driver. The U had the choice of Mack, Mack/Scania or Cummins engines of 180 to 375bhp and 5 to 18 forward gears. The C-series had a specially short bonnet and cab to allow it to couple to 40ft trailers yet remain within the 50ft overall limit.

An example of the new 4000/9000 range of 1966 with fibreglass hood (bonnet) and fenders (wings). Various gas (186 to 250bhp) and diesel (160 to 335bhp) engines were available.

A pair of Freightliners hauling 22-ton liquid tankers in the mid sixties. Freightliner trucks were marketed by White until 1977, having first appeared in 1938 as long haul rigs built to one operator's requirements.

Latest in White's medium weight and local delivery range is the Road Xpeditor2 4 × 2 and 6 × 4 range with steel tilt cab. This example has a 210bhp Caterpillar diesel, though engines of up to 322bhp are available in the range.

White treats its 'West Coast' models as a separate brand sold with the Western Star name. This is a 1977 example available with Cummins or Caterpillar engines of up to 425bhp. A high proportion of aluminium components including frames are available and 4 × 2, 4 × 4, 6 × 4 and 6 × 6 versions are produced.

Other US Makes

There are several current small specialist producers of trucks in America. Makes that specialized exclusively in garbage collection, like the Master Truck, are outside our scope, but some of the specialists, like Oshkosh, FWD, CCC and Walter, have also produced vehicles for normal highway use.

Various ingenious attempts to make 'compromise' highway and urban delivery trucks have been tried and we show the ingenious Coleman space van. In addition there was the Wolfwagon of around 1960, which was a self-contained Cummins 130bhp engined truck which could be joined up into a rigidly linked convoy with only one driver.

The following pages give a selection from the smaller firms, some (but not all) still in business at the end of the seventies. Examples of their models from the sixties and seventies are shown.

Autocar has been a division of the White Motor Co. since 1953, specializing in heavy-duty custom built trucks, often for the construction industry. Shown here is a 1967 tractive unit for conventional highway use at 38 tons gtw. Most road models at the time had Cummins 220 or 250bhp diesels. The photograph was taken at the Brussels Show with a Scania Vabis in the background.

In 1956 Brockway became an autonomous division of Mack Trucks but twenty years later went out of business following financial difficulties. Shown here is one of their last products, a 1975 model 457 TL available with Cummins, Caterpillar or Detroit diesels of 230 to 370bhp and 5 to 16 forward gears. Brockway remained faithful to gasoline engines well into the seventies, even introducing a new 200bhp gas engine in 1961.

CCC stands for Crane Carrier Company, which explains the firm's principal interests. However during the seventies it has broadened its range to include custom built trucks for other purposes. Shown is a 1976 Centurion low profile tilt-cab truck specifically designed for front end garbage loading. It was for a gvw of up to 68,000lbs and could have Caterpillar, Cummins or Detroit diesels.

Right Coleman was best known for off-road trucks and highway maintenance vehicles but in 1968 the firm announced this extraordinary prototype Spacevan, which unfortunately failed to attract buyers. The semi-trailer was locked rigidly to the tractor portion which had both 4-wheel drive and 4-wheel steering and a turning circle of 105 feet. Up to 15 forward gear ratios gave a top speed of 80mph and with second trailer the unladen weight was 16.3 tons. Power came from a Detroit 8V-71N diesel, developing 318bhp.

Highway have specialized in urban collection and delivery vehicles during the period, and shown here is a 1966 Compac Van. Body length ranged from 15–24ft, with gvw of 8–13 tons. The driver could step straight from his cab onto the loading platform, which could be raised or lowered to suit varying bay heights.

FWD specializes in custom-built off-highway vehicles, usually with all-wheel drive (its initial letters originally signified Four Wheel Drive). However in 1968 it introduced its 6 × 4 ForWarD Mover range for highway use. Shown are examples of the tilt-cab and conventional models for 25 tons gvw or 74,000lbs gtw in normal highway haulage. Cummins and Detroit engines of 220 to 320bhp were available with 10- to 16-speed transmission options.

Hendrickson are best known in worldwide trucking for their proprietary tandem axles supplied to various chassis manufacturers. However they also have a division producing custom built vehicles and this has been in business since 1915. Their on-highway vehicles are popular in the industrial area around Chicago, in their home state of Illinois. This is the H3 series 6 × 4 tractor of the early seventies.

Kenworth makes high quality line haul and special purpose vehicles and, as a member of the Paccar Group, is associated with Peterbilt. During the period it has had factories in America, Mexico and Canada, where a special range particularly suited to the logging industry was made. Shown is a 1966 6 × 4 aluminium tilt-cab model alongside a conventional (normal control) with forward hinging fibreglass hood (bonnet). A wide choice of proprietary engines and transmission options have been available. The external appearance of Kenworths remained like this at the end of the seventies.

Marmon-Herrington had made off-road vehicles for thirty years when in 1961 they introduced a Cummins 195bhp engined 6-wheel highway tractive unit. In 1963 the firm ceased production of all vehicles while continuing purely as a financial company. Since 1964 Marmon highway trucks have been built in small quantities by a new firm, the Marmon Motor Co. Shown is a 1975 model available with Cummins, Detroit or Caterpillar engines of up to 350bhp.

The E Series Oshkosh range of 1971 was for rigid, artic and drawbar trailer work on the highway and was available with 2 or 3 axles. They had tilt cabs and choice of Caterpillar engines between 200 and 270bhp. Similar models are assembled in South Africa and Australia.

Oshkosh has concentrated on custom made municipal and off-highway vehicles during the period and a typical 4 × 4 tipper is shown. It is a P-2025 with Caterpillar 250 or Cummins 220bhp diesels for 42,000lbs gvw. It had a 4-speed auxiliary gearbox and 5-speed main box. Visually identical vehicles were made throughout the sixties and early seventies.

Right Peterbilt has custom built high quality trucks in California throughout the period and has had certain affinities with Kenworth who, like them, are members of the Paccar group. This is a 1965 model 341 designed to carry 16.4 tons within the legal limit of 49,000lbs. It has an aluminium frame and Cummins 180bhp diesel with 5-speed main gearbox and 4-speed auxiliary.

Peterbilt cab-over-engine models have changed little in appearance over the past twenty years. This is a 1977 Model 352 tractive unit fitted with a 350bhp Cummins diesel.

Walter makes all-wheel drive vehicles for utilities; snow clearance, fire fighting, the construction industry and other special purposes. The nearest thing to a normal type of truck is their current Walter II chassis shown here, often used as a tractive unit or refuse collection vehicle. A feature of all Walters is the use of automatic locking and torque proportioning differentials, to give maximum wheel grip.

Studebaker-Packard stopped producing cars and trucks in America in 1964 but continued to assemble cars in Canada for a couple of years afterwards. One of their final attempts to break into the medium/heavy truck market was in 1961, when they introduced a 19,500 to 23,000lb gvw diesel range powered by 4-cylinder GM Detroit 130bhp engines. A 1961 example working at 41,000lbs gtw with a load of Studebaker cars is shown.

USSR, EASTERN EUROPE AND YUGOSLAVIA

Truck manufacturers in a socialist country have one thing in common — lack of competition. Imports are banned unless they are considered essential, the factories are controlled by the state and each factory produces a particular weight range that does not clash with other trucks made in the same country.

In the West, advances in technology have arisen as a result of each manufacturer's attempts to gain a sales advantage, and there has been hardly any equivalent of this in the socialist world. By the late sixties it was apparent that the Eastern European and Soviet designs were lagging behind those of the West, and socialist countries bought technology from outside.

Tatra of Czechoslovakia was notable as an exception to this pattern of buying from the West. As far back as the 1920s Tatra had distinguished themselves by introducing a very advanced backbone chassis using the swing axle suspension principle and originated by their designer Hans Ledwinka. They still use backbone chassis today.

The Polish Jelcz and Star factories have used Leyland, Steyr and Berliet patents. Hungary's Csepel was derived form Austria's Steyr and later West German MAN. Much of Romania's industry is derived from MAN as well, while many of the trucks are equipped with Mercedes and Perkins engines. Earlier, the influence had been ÖAF of Austria, and the German Krupp.

In East Germany, Robur and W50 trucks are built in factories inherited from before Germany was divided. Yugoslavia's FAP, Zastava and TAM designs stem from Saurer, Fiat and Magirus-Deutz respectively.

The products of Tatra, Skoda/Liaz, ROMAN and certain Soviet factories are sold in the West at competitive prices, often to all appearances below cost in order to gain foreign currency. But sales have not been in volumes that would pose a threat to the Western manufacturers. At the same time, production is increasing, and by 1980 annual production within the COMECON group of countries is expected to reach one million commercial vehicles.

This 1977 East German Robur LO 3000 has changed little since the 1950s. It has an air-cooled 4-cylinder 3345cc petrol engine derived from the Phänomen, which was produced until the division of Germany. Payload is 3 tonnes and it has 5 forward gears.

The Grube was superseded by the W50 some years ago, the latter now being East Germany's principle heavy vehicle type. This Grube S4000-1 dates from 1963 and was for 3.4-tonne loads. It had a 4-cylinder 6024cc diesel engine with 5 forward gears (2—5 with syncromesh).

A 1963 Hungarian Csepel D-455B with 4-cylinder 5.5-litre diesel engine developing 100bhp. It had 5 forward gears and was for 5-tonne loads.

Seen here at work in Switzerland in 1963 is a Škoda 706 RTS 9-tonne chassis with 11781cc 6-cylinder 170bhp diesel and 5-speed gearbox. Similar styling is used on current Škoda trucks, which are now made in the Liberecké Automobile Works, whose more recently developed models are known as LIAZ after the factory's initials.

Tatra specializes in all-wheel drive 3- and 4-axle trucks with the very unusual features of independent suspension and air-cooled engines. This is a 1967 138S3 model with 11762cc V-8 200bhp diesel and 10 forward gears. Payload was 11.75 tonnes and a 4 × 4 version was also offered. With few outward changes apart from a bigger air intake, the Tatra 6 × 6 was still being made in 1978. The larger models have forward control.

The latest product of Czechoslovakia's Liberecké factory, which began in 1967, is the LIAZ and here a 1977 tractive unit is shown working at 38 tonnes gtw. It has an 11.94-litre 350bhp 6-cylinder turbocharged diesel (British Holset turbocharger) with 2-range 5-speed gearbox, and is made to comply with Western European traffic regulations.

An all-wheel drive 1967 Praga V3S 3-tonner, with air cooled engine, which as its name implies was made in Prague. It is fitted with a 3-way tipping body and centre-pivot rear suspension. Praga is now best known for its gearboxes, which are used by LIAZ amongst others.

Romania's leading makers are RABA and SR, both of whom use diesel technology from the German MAN concern as well as other sources in the West. RABA are best known in the West for their axles, marketed by Eaton. This is a 1978 RABA U26.230 DFK 26-tonne gvw tipper with 230bhp 6-cylinder MAN-licence engine, inclined at 40° in the frame. Note the inverted front axle to give increased ground clearance.

Of obvious Magirus-Deutz origin is this 1977 TAM from Yugoslavia, though earlier designs came from Praga and Fiat. It has an 8-litre V-6 air-cooled diesel developing 125bhp, and is for 12 tonnes gvw.

Although this photograph dates from 1969 the GAZ still retained this curiously 'fifties' American styling all through the 1970s. This is a model 53A for 3.5 tonne loads, which carried its American inspiration still further by having a V-8 130bhp petrol engine.

The various Soviet types of truck are given the initial letters of their factory, hence the early sixties MAZ shown here comes from the Minsk Auto Zavodi (works). It was unusual in having a 2-stroke, 4-cylinder diesel engine, which developed 110bhp from 4.64 litres. Despite its archaic appearance it was fitted with a 5-speed synchromesh gearbox.

The KRAZ design goes back to the fifties and used an in-line 6-cylinder 2-stroke diesel of 180 or 205bhp until these were replaced by a V-8, 4-stroke 240bhp diesel. Used in the USSR for heavy haulage, construction and military work with 6 × 4 or 6 × 6 drive, it is also sold in Western Europe as the Belaz dump truck. The early seventies V-8 257 model shown could carry 14 tonnes and tow a 16-tonne gross trailer.

Just as the KRAZ lost its 2-stroke engine in the sixties, so did the MAZ, and here the revised 503A is shown in around 1972 with V-6, 200bhp diesel. Payload was 9 tonnes and the gearbox was similar to the earlier MAZ shown, though it no longer claimed to have synchromesh on bottom gear.

In the sixties there were a number of takeovers in the industry, Toyota acquiring Daihatsu and Hino, and Nissan/Datsun acquiring Prince. 1971 saw the American motor industry taking a close interest in Japan with the result that General Motors began to market Isuzu vehicles overseas, even selling them in Australia as Bedfords, while Chrysler bought a 15 per cent stake in Mitsubishi. An unusual feature of Japanese heavy trucks is the number of twin-steer 6-wheelers available.

Exhibited in Britain for the first time in 1978 was the USSR's new KAMAZ — the first truck built with a serious eye to Western markets. It borrowed technical know-how from GMC, Magirus-Deutz and Mack amongst others, and annual production of 150,000 was planned for 1980. The example shown is for 32.5 tonnes gcw (23 tonnes gvw as a rigid) and has a 210bhp V-8 diesel and 8-speed splitter gearbox.

Daihatsu cars and light trucks were amongst the first Japanese makes to be marketed in Europe in the late sixties, and this is their D200 2-ton truck with 2.3-litre 63bhp diesel engine on show at Brussels in 1969. In the previous year Japanese sales in Belgium had amounted to only 57 trucks, though this was just the thin end of the wedge. In 1968 Daihatsu were acquired by Toyota, though they retain their separate identity to this day.

JAPAN

From being unknown outside its own country in 1960, the Japanese truck industry has become a major exporter of light and medium trucks to many traditionally British and American markets. During the seventies it has developed increasingly heavy vehicles as well, and these are assembled in several countries that do not have an indigenous truck industry.

Isuzu, Mitsubishi and Hino are the principal heavy truck makers whilst nearly all the car firms also produce diminutive trucks which go up to about 4 tons capacity but would, in many cases, be rated for only half that by European manufacturers.

Another firm to be bought by Toyota, this time in 1967, was Hino. Shown is a TA model of 1964 with 8-litre 6-cylinder 155bhp diesel engine. It was destined for South America and carries lubricating equipment.

A Hino twin-steer 6-wheeler of 1963. This TC model had a tilt cab, 5-speed gearbox and 10,178cc 6-cylinder diesel engine developing 195bhp. It was for payloads of 10 tonnes.

As well as owning Daihatsu and Hino, Toyota has its own truck range of up to 4 tons capacity. This is their current Dyna, available with petrol or diesel engines of 76 to 93bhp, for 2- to 3-ton loads.

This Hino shows the 1976 styling adopted for the KM medium weight range models of mid sixties origin. This example has a 6-cylinder 4313cc 90bhp diesel engine and 5-speed gearbox.

A Toyota 6-tonner of the early sixties with 130bhp, 6.5-litre 6-cylinder diesel engine and 5-speed synchromesh gearbox (optional overdrive fifth if required). A 5-tonner with 5.9-litre 110bhp engine was also available.

An Isuzu TS540 all-wheel drive tipper chassis of 1962, for 5-tonne loads. It had a 6-cylinder 6126cc 125bhp diesel engine and 2-range, 4-speed gearbox. Similar styling was retained by Isuzu for its more rugged 2- and 3-axle models into the seventies.

A Titan 3700, the largest vehicle in the Mazda range of 1977. It had a 3.7-litre 100bhp diesel engine and was for 2—3.5-ton loads. Other outwardly similar versions could have 2-litre petrol or 2.7-litre diesel engines.

A current Isuzu TD 50 AD model with styling adopted in 1973. It is for 16 tonnes gvw and has a 6-cylinder 10.2-litre 195bhp diesel engine and 2-range, 4-speed gearbox. A forward control version is also produced.

This Mitsubishi Jupiter dates from 1964 and was available in 2-, 3- and 3½-ton capacity versions with 76bhp 4-cylinder petrol or 61bhp 4-cylinder 2199cc diesel or 6-cylinder 3299cc 85bhp diesel engines.

24

Mitsubishi's heavy models are marketed under the name Fuso and this is a 6W200R tractive unit for 80,000lbs gtw. It dates from approximately 1970 and has a 200bhp 6-cylinder diesel engine, all-wheel drive and a 2-range, 5-speed gearbox.

Nissan is the parent company of Datsun and their trucks are sold with the Nissan name. This is a 1966 model 681 with choice of 3706cc petrol or diesel engines, the latter developing 125bhp. It was rated as a 5-tonner with 4-speed gearbox, and 6-tonner with 5 speeds. The same vehicle was made in Taiwan under the name Yueloong. In 1966 Nissan took over Prince Motors, who had formerly made Mikado light trucks.

A Fuso T810 of 1975 with massive 260in wheelbase. It was for 33,265lbs gvw. Various 4- and 6-wheel models (including twin-steer 6-wheelers) were available with this cab and could have diesel engines of 132 to 265bhp output.

UNITED KINGDOM

The UK has lost many of its individual manufacturers as a result of mergers which took place in the sixties and seventies, but in terms of volume it is still one of the world's 'big four' truck producers.

The sixties opened with the arrival of the famous TK Bedford, and then in 1962 the American idea of tilt cabs was introduced on Foden trucks, soon afterwards spreading to most other British manufacturers, reaching the mass produced class with BMC in 1964.

Turbochargers were introduced with some big proprietary engines in the early sixties, and were taken up by Ford's 'heavies' in 1968.

The 1964 *Construction and Use Regulations* led to a jump in maximum weight from 24 to 32 tons; and legal speed went up to 40mph. These new operating conditions favoured an influx of foreign vehicles which were already designed to these requirements.

The new regulations brought more business for the makers of the more powerful proprietary engines, with consequent expansion in that sector of the British industry — notably by Cummins. At the same time the American motor components industry invested heavily in the old Maudslay and Thornycroft factories, which thus grew into major suppliers of transmission equipment.

More dollars flowed in to add Seddon Atkinson to the list of American-owned British truck makers: Ford, Bedford and Dodge (until the latter became French-owned in 1978).

At the end of the seventies, Foden and ERF were the only two truck makers as such who remained independent of foreign ownership, in the company of several thriving specialist firms, and of course the giant quasi-nationalized British Leyland, who made more heavy trucks than anyone else in the British industry and at the end of the period launched a new range for the 1980s.

AEC

AEC had joined forces with Crossley and Maudslay in 1948 and had taken over Thornycroft in 1962, the year in which they in turn were bought by Leyland Motors. They gradually lost their identity as more and more Leyland components (including the Ergomatic cab from 1964) were fitted, and the AEC name had disappeared from trucks (though not coaches) by 1977. The Leyland Marathon was however made at AEC's Southall, Middlesex factory until 1979.

This 1960 AEC Mammoth Major 24-ton gvw tipper has the famous AEC 9.6-litre 128bhp 6-cylinder diesel with 5-speed and reverse constant-mesh gearbox and Maudslay axles (Maudslay had ceased to make their own vehicles in the fifties, though at one time had been handling the assembly of the Mammoth Major).

This is a Reiver working in South Africa in 1964. It has a Leyland 0.400 diesel developing 125bhp and a 6-speed gearbox. The cab was Leyland's Vista Vue, made by Motor Panels, which continued on several 'no frills' Albion models long after the new Ergomatic cab appeared in 1964.

Atkinson

Atkinson had been a small maker of high quality, assembled diesel trucks since the early thirties, and from the late fifties had diversified into special purpose off-road vehicles in addition to their normal haulage models. They made Omega desert tractors, dump trucks, heavy haulage models, crane carriers, snow clearers etc. In 1970 they were bought by Seddon who were in turn acquired by the American firm International Harvester in 1974. Thereafter, Seddon and Atkinson vehicles became Seddon Atkinsons and the Atkinson factory has made the rationalized steel cabbed 400 series since 1975, over 5000 of which were sold in the first three years.

Albion

One of Leyland's first acquisitions (in 1951) was Albion Motors, whose name finally disappeared in 1972 although their Glasgow factory remains busy producing certain Leyland truck models to this day.

Right In an attempt to shake off their traditional image, Atkinson showed their new View-Line cab in 1966 and used it as a demonstrator on a Silver Knight T.3266C model with Cummins NH250 engine. The same vehicle was later sold, and entered service with R. Hall of Sidcup in 1967. Not many View-Line equipped vehicles were sold, though later examples had rather neater frontal treatment using a fibreglass radiator surround, as on conventional models, which did away with the assortment of grilles shown here.

Two Gardner 150bhp engines Atkinson tractive units with articulated trailers about to embark on the M1 Motorway in the early sixties. The familiar wrap-around windscreen and fibreglass cab had first appeared in 1958 and survived in modified form until soon after the International takeover.

Austin, Morris and BMC

Austin and Morris had merged in 1952 to form the British Motor Corporation and rationalization of their truck ranges had taken place during the 1950s. Most models were available with either nameplate and occasionally just BMC until 1968, when BMC became the correct title for all the heavy models. In 1968 Leyland merged with British Motor Holdings, which was the parent company of BMC, and this led to further rationalization. Production of the truck ranges was transferred from the Midlands to Bathgate in Scotland in 1970, henceforth under the Leyland name.

The traditional exposed radiator had long been an Atkinson feature but by the time this Gardner 180bhp engined 26-ton gvw Defender tipper was made in 1971 it had become a fibreglass moulding concealing a modern radiator in place of the former cast aluminium design. This example has the usual fibreglass cab, which combined with a Nevilloy body, helped to keep the unladen weight below 9½ tons and allow a 16½-ton payload.

Launched in November 1959, the 'threepenny bit' BMC FG cab was soon to be seen on thousands of urban distribution vehicles where driver visibility and ease of access (the doors opened within the width of the body) were a boon. This is the Austin T200 version of 1960 for 2-ton loads with choice of BMC 4-litre petrol or 3.4-litre diesel engines. Up to 65mph/15mpg and 45mph/25mpg were claimed respectively for these engines in laden vehicles. The FG has lived on and its cab is still used today on many Leylands supplied to the distributive trades.

A popular conversion was for specialist engineers to add rear trailing or front steering axles to increase the payload of cheap, mass produced trucks. This 1961 7-ton Austin 702 has a twin-steer conversion by the Primrose 3rd Axle Co. to increase its payload by 50 per cent yet was expected to get by on its usual 5.1-litre 6-cylinder BMC diesel engine and 4-speed constant-mesh gearbox. The cab on this model was common to both the largest Morris and Austins and had first appeared in 1958.

A contemporary publicity artist's impression of the Morris WF K100 5-ton capacity tipper of 1964. A similar cab had been used on Morris and Austin normal control vehicles for many years but this was the first year of twin headlights and one piece windscreens. 4-litre petrol or 5.1-litre diesel engines were fitted and the model was primarily popular overseas, in countries where overall length was less critical than easy engine accessibility, and where three abreast seating was preferred.

A Perkins V-8 engined, 16-ton gvw BMC Mastiff of 1969 operated by Kennings (one of the country's largest Morris distributors) on their domestic fuel delivery fleet. Austin and Morris heavy commercial vehicles were known as BMC between 1968 and 1970, when following the merger with Leyland they were renamed Leyland Redlines (to differentiate them from the traditional Blueline 'genuine' Leylands). The cab used on all these models is based on the FJ design, which first appeared in 1964 and was the first tilt cab from one of the mass produced truck makers.

Bedford

During the fifties Bedford had become the largest producer of trucks in Britain, and indeed the world's most successful truck exporter. Despite its American GMC backing, most Bedfords since the early thirties had been British in design and concept and the important new TK of 1960 was no exception. Normal control models (especially for export) continued to be made alongside the TK as well as the 4 × 4 which for many years retained the former 'Big Bedford' cab. In 1974 Bedford moved into the heavy league with its Detroit 2-stroke engined (Bedford diesel in the smallest) TM range for 17 to 42 tonnes gross weight.

Normally seen as an artic unit or rigid for high-speed drawbar trailer work, the Bedford TM is also being tried as a site vehicle. This is the 1976 prototype 6 × 4 tipper able to gross up to 30 tonnes. It has a Detroit 6V-71 diesel developing 221bhp and a specially shortened wheelbase of 147 inches (3734mm).

Right An appropriately registered Bedford TK at work with the Forestry Commission in 1962. The TK was launched at the London Commercial Motor Show in 1960 as a range of 3- to 7½-ton rigids and 8-, 10- and 12-ton artics using various 4- and 6-cylinder petrol and diesel engines of 64–133bhp. It had an advanced cab, still in production in 1979, in which the engine was placed over and behind the front axle to permit access from behind. The resulting low floor height was an added improvement. Weight distribution was nearer to that of a normal control vehicle, which helped to reduce steering effort, and visibility was first class.

Commer, Dodge and Karrier

Commer was bought by the Rootes brothers in the late twenties and Karrier in the mid thirties. After the Second World War Vulcan and Tilling-Stevens joined them, both of which were soon phased out, the latter leaving as its legacy the famous 2-stroke engine used in many Commers in the fifties and sixties. In 1964 the American Chrysler Corp. began to buy into the Rootes Group and had obtained complete control by 1973. Chrysler owned Dodge, who had made trucks in Britain since 1933, and in 1976 the Commer name was discontinued, all vehicles then being known as Dodges, apart from a few Karriers for municipal duties. In 1978 the French Peugeot-Citroën group bought up all Chrysler's European assets.

A 1964 Karrier Bantam in unusual guise. Normally seen as a refuse collector, gully emptier or 2-ton capacity tipper, this version was used as a small artic for transporting bus shelters. It had a 2.26-litre 4-cylinder 56bhp diesel engine and crew cab. Since 1974 and the arrival of the Commer Commando, Karriers have used a version of the Commando's cab.

Diesel Dodges were sold in the sixties and seventies on an image of cheap ruggedness and have always used proprietary engines. These 1965 9-tonners have the familiar Perkins 6.354 120bhp 6-cylinder diesels, the first automotive Perkins engine to have direct injection when launched. This style of Dodge had been around since 1958 and these examples were the largest rigids to be produced by the firm up to that time. A proprietary Motor Panels design was used, which also appeared on contemporary Leylands, Albions, etc.

The Commer Maxiload CE16 was nearing the end of its production run when this example was made in 1971, its styling and enlarged cab having first appeared in 1962. It had amongst the last 2-stroke engines to be offered in British trucks before the arrival of the Detroit-engined Bedford TMs. However, unlike the conventionally built Detroit, the Commer unit bristled with eccentricities, including 6 opposed pistons working in 3 cylinders. It developed 125bhp from only 3.52 litres.

In 1965 attempts were made to integrate the Dodge and Commer ranges, which resulted in a lot of badge engineering but not much in the way of new models, apart from the Dodge 500 series with the new cab style shown here. Just as the marketing men envisaged Commer Walk-Thru and medium weight models with Dodge names, so their artists did the same transformation with the Dodge, as this Perkins 6.354 engined model clearly shows.

The Commer Commando range came out early in 1974 with this new cab and choice of Perkins or Mercedes-Benz diesels or Chrysler petrol engines. This is the RG 16 tipper for 16 tons gvw. When the Commer name was phased out in 1976 it became the Dodge Commando, although occasional versions have since been sold under the Karrier name.

Dennis

Dennis had dropped out of the heavy vehicle market in the 1950s and was concentrating on municipal and local delivery vehicles as well as the Pax medium weight range. In 1964 they introduced the Maxim maximum capacity 4-wheel 16-ton, and 6-wheel 22-ton gvw models and their articulated derivatives, but these were not a commercial success and thereafter the firm concentrated increasingly on fire appliances and municipal vehicles, while the Pax lived on into the seventies as the DB 15.5 and Defiant prime mover.

In 1972 Dennis was acquired by Hestair, who have helped to revitalize the firm, and new bus models are made with the promise of steel-cabbed goods vehicles to follow. In the meantime a fibreglass-cabbed Delta II 16-tonner appeared in 1978.

The Dennis Maxim appeared first in 1964 with the American inspired but Darlington made Cummins V-8 185bhp diesel engine, Dennis 5-speed constant-mesh gearbox and fibreglass cab modified from that used on the Pax V. From 1966 the Perkins 170bhp V-8 and Fuller 5-speed synchromesh gearbox were available, and this example was suitable for a gtw of up to 30 tons.

ERF

ERF had built up a similar 'quality' reputation to that of Atkinson with its assembled trucks using Gardner engines in the fifties, and like Atkinson was prepared to make small batches of special-purpose models alongside its general haulage range. Thus it built dump trucks, 6 × 6 desert tractors from 1962, and from 1966 special fire appliance chassis with Rolls-Royce and Perkins engines. It was the pioneer British user of fail-safe spring emergency/parking brakes in 1966.

In 1962 ERF had offered the first British heavy truck with fully automatic gearbox and had used disc brakes even earlier on its dump trucks. An increasing number of Cummins and Rolls-Royce engines were used from the early sixties, alongside the popular Gardner engines. In 1970 the rationalized A-Range appeared and in 1974 came the B-series, with its new steel framed plastics cab. A lighter M model became available in 1978.

In 1962 came ERF's equally stylish LV cabbed models, initially with the same angled badge as on the earlier models, but by 1965, when this Gardner 150bhp-engined 8-wheeler was made, with the lettering shown here.

The ERF B-Series is available as 4-, 6- and 8-wheel rigids and 4- and 6-wheel artic units. This 1975 example has a Cummins 232bhp diesel engine and is for 32-ton gtw operation. A similar cab is used on the 16-ton gvw M model of 1978, which uses Gardner or Dorman engines of 160bhp. The B-Series is widely used in Britain, with annual production of around 3000 units, and sells well abroad, no mean achievement for a relatively small independent manufacturer.

It is astonishing to realize that the modern cab styling of this 1960 ERF first appeared as early as 1954, though then with single headlights. It showed what a relatively small manufacturer could achieve with the 'new' material, fibreglass. This example, shown at Dover, is equipped with a 150bhp Gardner 6LX diesel, and drawing a low-load trailer and Caterpillar bound for Belgium.

Foden

During the sixties and seventies Foden has been one of the most enterprising independent truck manufacturers, and has built a far higher proportion of the components for its trucks than is common. In the right hands its 2-stroke diesels have performed well and only went out of production in 1977, though few had been fitted as original equipment in trucks after the late sixties. Gardner engines had been generally more popular and, from the sixties, Cummins began to be fitted in increasing quantities. These were joined by Rolls-Royce engines (used in some dump trucks from the fifties) and a few Leylands, at a time when Leyland had a small financial interest in the firm.

Foden tried a number of ingenious ideas in the sixties, including twin-steer artics; the first tilt cab to be available from a British chassis manufacturer, in 1962; 8-wheel load-carrying models hauling semi trailers, in 1964; and half cabs and full cabs with forward-angled windscreens for road models, from 1968.

A wide range of general haulage models, dump trucks, crane carriers, and from 1973, military vehicles have been made by Foden and in 1974 one of the most modern factories in the business was opened. The development costs of this led to financial difficulties and a near Government takeover, but the firm is now back on its feet with a £10 million NATO order and, from 1977, new Fleetmaster and Haulmaster artic models.

Foden built similar chassis with low-level cabs as the basis of truck-mounted cranes and this 1965 example is one of a small number built to carry girders of over 50ft length in safety. The engine cover can just be seen at the front of the platform.

This cab shape appeared in 1962 and was the first tilt cab to be produced by a British chassis manufacturer. The mid sixties example shown has a Gardner engine and Foden 12-speed gearbox, though the Foden Dynamic 4.8-litre 2-stroke was also available developing 175bhp, or 225bhp when turbocharged.

Foden has long-standing connections in Australia and South Africa and this 210bhp FRTU 6/40 heavy haulage tractor is shown at work in New South Wales in 1963. The traditional radiator was used for increased coolant capacity and robustness. Note the oversize air cleaner intake at the nearside front.

The enormous amount of time taken to develop the Concorde is brought home when one realizes that this Foden, with 12,000-gallon John Thompson refuelling tank and 850gpm delivery pump, was one of three built to work in conjunction with the supersonic airliner as long ago as 1968. The complete unit is 56ft long and therefore illegal for road use.

Right The Foden Fleetmaster and Haulmaster were introduced in 1977 and shared similar Motor Panels steel tilt cabs which differed mainly in grille treatment and windscreen (divided on the Haulmaster). However under the skin they are a very different concept in that the Fleetmaster has more power (Cummins or Rolls-Royce 290bhp) and proprietary transmission components to simplify maintenance on the European mainland, whilst the cheaper Haulmaster uses mainly Foden components and Cummins, Gardner or Rolls-Royce diesels of 180–265bhp. A fibreglass and aluminium cab with similar styling was also available for 1979.

Foden has often been the rigid 8-wheeler market leader and here we see a 30 tons gvw RR 22/32 model of 1976 with Rolls-Royce 220bhp 6-cylinder diesel, 8-speed gearbox and double-drive rear bogie. It is fitted with a Pesci self-stacker and has a plastic tilt cab.

Ford

British Ford trucks have come a long way since 1960 and with the arrival of the Transcontinental, built in Amsterdam in 1975, they have been able to offer trucks of every payload capacity on the British market and are frequently the largest supplier, with Leyland and Bedford close behind. The familiar Thames Trader gave way in 1965 to the D-Series (marketed as a Ford, not Thames, for the first time) with its tilt cab, which is still their most popular medium-weight truck. Through much of the period bonnetted trucks have also been built, though these are primarily for export.

Right The Thames Trader gave way to the D-series in 1965, which in improved form is still with us in 1979. From the outset it had a steel tilt cab with printed circuit instrumentation and initially covered the 2- to 8-ton payload range plus artics. They were powered by new engines derived from the old 4D and 6D using similar blocks, but with dry cylinder liners. The example shown is a 1965 D750 (7.5-ton payload, 115bhp diesel with option of 149bhp petrol engine and 4- or 5-speed gearbox) used for carrying empty whisky casks.

A 1960 Thames Trader 108in wheelbase tipper with 6cu yd Pilot body being loaded with 7 tons of soil at Ascot racecourse. This largest rigid Thames was available with 6-cylinder petrol or diesel engines of 109 and 100bhp respectively. The familiar semi-forward control Thames had sold well in the fifties, accounting in some years for 1 in 4 registrations in its weight range.

One of the new style of normal control Thames Traders on test in 1962. This is the 4-ton model with 4D engine developing 65bhp from 3.6 litres and 4-speed gearbox (synchromesh on all but first). This cab styling had come from Ford of Germany and was made in Britain by the Pressed Steel Co. Ltd. Top speed was 47mph and fuel consumption around 20mpg. With the end of the Thames Trader the normal control range was renamed the Ford K-Series.

Guy

Guy Motors had always done well with light and medium weight commercial vehicles but in the fifties faced fearsome competition from the mass producers, and following the death of their founder in 1957 they were soon in serious financial difficulties. Guy was rescued in 1961 by Jaguar Cars Ltd. who concentrated on their heavy range of fibreglass-cabbed models, which had first appeared in 1958. In 1964, the steel-cabbed Big J range appeared, though some of the fibreglass-cab models continued into 1967. With the subsequent merger of Jaguar and BMC the Big J would have been the cornerstone of the combine's heavy vehicle plans. However the Leyland takeover in 1968 changed this and the Big J continued as a basic 'no frills' vehicle alongside the more sophisticated Leylands right up to its end in 1979.

The Big J tilt-cab range initially used Cummins vee engines as standard, with the option of Gardner and AEC diesels for the home market. Jaguar intended to produce 200 and 170bhp V-6 engines under licence, from Cummins, but instead they bought them from Cummins' British factory. The Big J 22-ton gvw rigid could have Cummins 170bhp or 152 to 164bhp AEC engines and this example dates from 1968.

Typical of the fibreglass-cabbed range that first appeared in 1958 is this 1965 Invincible 8-wheeler, which remained in production for a time following the announcement of the Big J range at the previous year's Commercial Motor Show in London. It has a Gardner 6LX 150bhp diesel. Another contemporary Guy 8-wheeler was the Warrior Light Eight, which, as its name implied, was of lighter build and used the Gardner 6LW 112bhp diesel or the AEC AV470 7.7-litre engine, which developed 125bhp.

International

Although the International Harvestor Co. was well known as a truck producer in the USA it came as something of a surprise when its British farm machinery factory at Doncaster began to produce Loadstar trucks with Perkins engines in 1965. A fair number were sold and a forward control version was planned for 1967. However the whole project was inadequately profitable and ended within a couple of years.

When International were next heard of in British trucking circles it was because of their purchase of Seddon-Atkinson in 1974.

A 1966 British built International 1700 Loadstar tipper. Other versions were the 1600 and 1800, figures which indicated a tenth of the rear axle load capacity in pounds. They had 131bhp Perkins engines and either 4- or 5-speed synchromesh gearboxes. The example shown is the 151in wheelbase model and six other versions from 139–217in were available.

Leyland

Leyland has been Britain's largest producer of medium to heavy diesel trucks in the past two decades. In the sixties it expanded enormously with the acquisition of AEC/Thornycroft in 1962, followed by Bristol, Rover/Alvis and then Aveling-Barford, followed in 1968 by a merger of far-reaching consequences with British Motor Holdings, who controlled Austin, Morris, Guy and Daimler commercial vehicles.

The sixties opened with Leyland's new Power Plus engine range and was followed by their familiar Michelotti-styled Ergomatic tilt cab in 1964. Then came the Fixed Head 500 engine range in 1968 at a time when experiments with Leyland turbines looked as if these might lead to the power plant of the future.

Throughout the period the various makes taken over by Leyland (including their earlier Scammell and Albion acquisitions) have generally been rationalized and renamed Leylands. The firm was able to enter the mass production truck market with the Leyland Redlines (formerly BMC) in 1970 and in 1973 unveiled their new top weight Marathon range. Following a liquidity crisis in 1975 the corporation came to depend heavily on government finance and to be subject to planning control by the National Enterprise Board.

Unfamiliar to British eyes but sold widely in the Middle East from 1964 onwards was this variety of bonnetted Super Comet. It used the same Airflow Streamlines cab as found on certain Dodge and Commer models and on the Baron export chassis. This example was one of 2000 supplied to Iran with 125bhp Leyland Power Plus 0.400 engines and 5-speed constant-mesh gearboxes with 2-speed back axles. The gvw was conservatively rated at 14 tons.

Under the Austin-Morris heading we examined how these products became BMC and were then produced in Scotland as Leyland Redlines. This is a 1970 16-ton gvw Perkins V-8 engined Mastiff carrying 10 tons of animal food in an 820cu.ft tank with a pneumatic discharge system.

In 1964 the Beaver and many of its Leyland stablemates acquired the Ergomatic tilt cab. This is a Beaver made earlier in the year with the previous fixed cab. It could carry almost 9 tons and had a 140bhp Leyland 6-cylinder diesel engine.

Although this Super Hippo is shown in use in Sabah (North Borneo) in 1963 the origins of this model go back much further and was produced until 1979 for very arduous overseas service. This example carried 30-ton loads of logs and had the 0.680 Power Plus engine developing 200bhp. A 7-speed crawler/overdrive gearbox was fitted with hub reduction rear axles to reduce torque loading on the rear differentials.

Left The well known Ergomatic tilt cab (fixed on some later models) made for Leyland by Sankeys of Wellington, first appeared in 1964 and in restyled form was still with us into 1979 when a new shape appeared. Of all the dozens of different models that used it, we show an early prototype of Leyland's gas turbine truck, which with striking styling provided later by Rovers was unveiled in 1968. The example shown has a 150bhp Rover gas turbine whereas the pre-production examples were 400bhp 6-wheelers. Volume production was envisaged in the early seventies but after only a handful had been supplied for operator evaluation, the energy crisis dealt the project a mortal blow.

Scammell

Scammell has been a Leyland subsidiary since 1955 and has tended to be the specialist in small batch production of export and heavy duty vehicles. Alongside these it has made mechanical horses (a 4-wheel version with Standard Atlas cab was tried from 1962, the 3-wheel Townsman of 1964 being the last new design) and regular haulage vehicles using a higher proportion of outside proprietary parts than other Leyland companies (with the erstwhile exception of Guy and of recent Marathons). It has managed to retain its own name, although the bonnetted Contractor launched in 1964 and Commander of 1978 are often marketed as Leylands, and the Michelotti-styled forward control glass-fibre cab, new in 1962, is still unique to Scammell. In the mid seventies the production of Thornycroft's remaining models was transferred to the Scammell factory.

The Leyland Ergomatic cab was restyled with horizontal ribs across its front panels at the time the new fixed cylinder head 500 series engine was launched in 1968 in the Lynx and Bison. In 1974 it had another facelift as shown here on a 1975 Octopus 8-wheeler, Leylands first rigid 8 since the sixties and designed as a replacement for the AEC Mammoth Major 8. Initially a 200bhp fixed head engine was used but later a non turbocharged version of the Marathon AEC designed TL12 engine (the 230bhp L12) was available. The low unladen weight allowed over 21 tons to be carried within the 30-ton gvw limit.

The Highwayman name, for Scammell's famous normal control road haulage model, was adopted in 1955 and it continued right through to the sale of the last in 1970, to Sri Lanka, by which time the space lost by not placing the cab over the engine was too valuable a commodity to be continued, even if it did provide easier engine access and a pleasing appearance. This 1963 example is for 30-ton gtw operation and has a Gardner 6LX engine (Leyland power was also available).

The Constructor first appeared in 1952 and is still made today in developed form as the Super Constructor 6 × 6 for on-off-road operation at 102 tons gtw. This Constructor, in use in the Middle Eastern oilfields in the mid sixties, had the option of Leyland 161 or 200bhp, Rolls Royce 185 or 200bhp or Cummins 173 or 212bhp diesels with 12 forward and 2 reverse gears. Its gvw was a 46½ tons and its payload around 30 tons.

The Trunker II which appeared in 1965 (1967 model shown) used the Michelotti designed fibreglass cab first seen on the Routeman II 8-wheeler in 1962 and the Handyman III (a sort of forward control Highwayman) in 1964. Whereas the original Trunker of 1960 had been a 6-wheeler of conventional wheel layout (though single rear tyres) but with Leyland cab and horizontal Gardner engine, the Mk II had a second steering axle placed immediately ahead of the driven rear axle and a vertical engine, in this case a Gardner 180bhp diesel.

Left The Crusader is now generally seen as a 4 × 2 artic prime mover for 32 tons gtw with Rolls-Royce diesel, though 6 × 4 versions are made, primarily for export. When the model first appeared in 1968 with its Motor Panels steel cab it was planned as a tractive unit for the 44 tons gtw limit believed to be impending. In fact the limit was not raised from 32 tons so the 290bhp Detroit 2-stroke (Cummins 300bhp V-8 or AEC 272bhp V-8 optional) tractor was seldom seen in Britain. It had 10 forward gears and a top speed of 55mph.

Seddon

Seddon was very successful with its competitively priced medium trucks as well as more specialized maximum capacity artics. It came close to merging with Dennis in 1963, and in 1967 formed a joint company with the makers of German Deutz vehicles which resulted in a few Deutz engined Seddons and the assembly of Magirius-Deutz trucks in Britain until 1970. In 1970 Seddon joined forces with quality heavy vehicle maker Atkinson and in 1974 the combined group was bought by International Harvester.

In 1964 Seddon had amazed the mass producers of medium trucks by introducing its cheap and well made steel-cabbed and Perkins-engined 13/4 range. This was replaced in 1975 by the 200 International powered range which used a lowered version of the 400 cab shown in the Atkinson entry.

New in 1964 was the 13/4 (13 tons gvw, 4-wheeler) with its steel Supa-cab made by Motor Panels. It had a Perkins 6.354 engine developing 113bhp and 5-speed David Brown gearbox. This is a 1965 version with Primrose third axle conversion to enable it to gross 18 tons. In 1965 a Perkins V-8 engined 16/4 rigid and 28/4 tractive unit of similar appearance to the 13/4 appeared. In modified form this style of Seddon continued to be made after the arrival of the 200 Series in 1975, primarily for municipal duties.

This attractively styled fibreglass cab was used on the 6- to 7-ton model and its artic derivative from 1957. This is a 1961 example with Perkins 112bhp diesel towing a Boden trailer fitted with a 10- to 12-ton container. Until the arrival of the Perkins 6.354 in 1960 many medium weight Seddons were Leyland powered, though afterwards this make of engine, as well as Gardners, was reserved primarily for maximum capacity 4- and 8-wheelers.

This style of fibreglass Seddon cab was used on the largest models from 1961 onwards and here we see a 1966 30/4/6LX, this model designation signifying 30 tons gtw, 4-wheel, Gardner 6LX engine (a similar type was available with AEC engine).

Thornycroft

Thornycroft continued to offer their normal 4-, 6- and 8-wheel goods models until their takeover by AEC in 1961, soon after which all were discontinued. Thereafter the firm concentrated on gearboxes and special purpose military, off-road and export vehicles. Following the Leyland takeover, many of these special vehicles (especially the Antar and Big Ben heavy tractors) clashed with the Scammell range and were discontinued. Thornycroft production moved to the Scammell factory in 1970 and only the Nubian 6 × 6 fire/crash tender remained plus a new Bushmaster tractor introduced in 1970 and based on the AEC 690 Dumptruck. In 1977 the name Thornycroft finally disappeared and its surviving model became a Leyland or Scammell Nubian. In 1978 the design was discontinued in favour of a new rear engined layout.

When this 6 × 6 Nubian with workshop body was supplied to Ceylon in 1961 the Nubian was usually built as an airport crash tender with an 8-cylinder Rolls-Royce petrol engine. However this example had a 130bhp Thornycroft diesel engine and weighed around 15 tons with all its engineering equipment aboard (which included a 2-ton crane, 8½in lathe, generator, air compressor, electric tools and welding set).

The Argyle Motor Manufacturing Co. of East Kilbride, Scotland was formed in 1968 to make 16-ton gvw 4-wheelers. Their vehicles had a similar specification to contemporary Seddons with Motor Panels cabs and Perkins 6.354 engines. Several dozen were sold before the firm went out of business in the mid seventies, finding that it could not compete on price with the bigger makers and could not persuade enough Scots to buy it on patriotic grounds.

Other British Makes

As well as the major makes already listed there have been a number of other small firms in business during the period making a variety of trucks, usually for very specialized purposes, including off-road vehicles, which are outside the scope of this book.

In 1962/3 Norde made a few Cummins 262bhp engined high speed Motorway artics as well as some Bedford TK cabbed general haulage models with rubber suspension; Jensen made the German Tempo under licence for a year or two into the sixties but had given up making its own trucks; Rowe continued to make its Meadows engined Hillmaster trucks in Cornwall until 1963; Lomount carried on from Rotinoff as a maker of heavy haulage tractors until about the same time; and TVW made the last few of its trucks from left over Sentinel spares in 1960; Bristol trucks were still available to the nationalized sector of the road transport industry until about 1965 (Bristol has survived as a PSV maker within the Leyland group). Examples of some of the other makes in the past twenty years are now shown.

Unipower were best known for their timber tractors and nowadays specialize in 4 × 4 airport crash tenders (as part of the AC Cars group since 1977). In 1971 they introduced the Invader general purpose 4 × 4 chassis and here we see it as a 28-ton gtw artic, able to work on rough construction sites yet maintain 50mph on the road. It had a Perkins V-8 170bhp diesel, Eaton 5-speed synchro gearbox and Thornycroft transfer box. In most European countries 4 × 4 site vehicles are commonplace but the Unipower was not a commercial success in this form in Britain.

41

After building a prototype in 1959, Baron Motors announced its simple and basic Perkins 6.354 engined trucks in 1964 for tough overseas service. The cab came from Airflow Streamlines who supplied similar types to Commer, Dodge and export Leyland Comets. Rated as a 5/6 tonner the Baron was intended primarily for overseas assembly using British proprietary components. Unfortunately its success was short-lived in the face of Japanese competition and lack of finance.

WEST GERMANY

There has been tremendous consolidation in the German truck industry in the past twenty years, with the stronger firms taking over the weaker to increase output and the number of individual manufacturers reducing year by year. Germany has also had an enlightened attitude towards large trucks, permitting 38 tonnes gtw from 1965 but at the same time making sure that these did not hamper other traffic by insisting on a minimum of 6bhp per ton.

Mercedes-Benz is the biggest maker of trucks and one of the world's largest producers of diesel vehicles today. MAN and Magirus-Deutz have commercial or technical links with several other manufacturers in Europe; MAN is about to move into a lighter weight range and VW into a heavier one, with a pooled design of medium weight trucks for the eighties. Several small specialist manufacturers thrive, but such once famous names as Borgward, Krupp, Hanomag and Henschel have disappeared.

MAN

MAN has long had a reputation for very high grade diesel engineering and in the past twenty years it has supplied technical expertise to Saviem in France, various Eastern European countries, ÖAF in Austria and even Mercedes-Benz and VW in its home country. In 1971 it took over rival heavy vehicle maker Büssing (it had owned a half share since 1967) and collaborated with VW to make a joint range of medium weight trucks in 1979.

Shelvoke and Drewry had concentrated on municipal vehicles, with Leyland or Perkins diesels, throughout the past twenty years until, in 1975, they increased their scope with a department to build special vehicles, often for off-road use. Shown here is an earlier special production, a 1967 6-wheel version of the largest Leyland 115bhp engined T Series refuse collection chassis, fitted with street washing equipment.

This 38-tonne MAN 14212/230 DFS tractor could have 9.659-litre 212bhp or 230bhp 6-cylinder diesel engines. It dates from 1967.

Available with forward or, as shown here, semi forward control layout this MAN 13.168 of 1974 had a 168bhp 5-cylinder diesel and 6-speed gearbox. The forward control cab style is shown on the Saviem page.

Magirus-Deutz

Magirus-Deutz is second only to Mercedes-Benz in terms of sales in Germany. In the early sixties it was overtaken by MAN and by 1967 their respective market shares were 15 and 20 per cent compared with nearly 50 per cent held by Mercedes, but it managed to fight back to second place in the seventies.

Magirus-Deutz sold trucks in Britain in the early sixties and formed a short-lived joint company with Seddon in 1967 to build them here. They were members of the 'Club of Four' (with Volvo, DAF, Saviem) who jointly designed medium trucks in the mid seventies. In 1974 Magirus-Deutz joined forces with Fiat, OM, Lancia and Unic to create IVECO (Industrial Vehicles Corporation) and there has subsequently been considerable interchange of designs and components between the member companies. They are keen exponents of air-cooled engined commercial vehicles and have used them almost exclusively for 40 years (they made a gas turbine truck in 1968).

Right A 1966 200D 22B 6 × 4 mixer chassis (200bhp, 22 tons gvw) of the type assembled in Britain by a joint Seddon and Magirus-Deutz factory.

A mid sixties 38-tonne gtw Magirus-Deutz with air-cooled V-8 Deutz 235bhp diesel.

1976 Magirus-Deutz 232 refuse collector for 19 tonnes gvw has air-cooled 232bhp V-8 diesel.

A 1969 LP1632 demonstrates its new tilt cab. This model was for drawbar trailer work at 38 tonnes gtw and had a new V-10 320bhp diesel engine designed in association with MAN.

Mercedes-Benz

Mercedes-Benz have retained their dominant position in the German medium to heavy truck field in the past twenty years and have greatly strengthened their performance at the light end with the acquisition of Hanomag-Henschel almost ten years ago. They have technical links with MAN and with Steyr in Austria and assembly plants in several overseas countries, notably South America and the Middle East.

Although still seen on certain heavy duty, off-road models in 1978 the cab design shown on this LA 1620 model of 1963 had been around since 1958. This 4 × 4 tipper has a payload of 9 tonnes and a 160bhp 6-cylinder diesel.

A 1974 6 × 6 2626AK tipper for 26 tonnes gvw. It had a 256bhp V-8 diesel and the 'New Generation' cab that spread to much of the Mercedes-Benz range from the mid seventies.

Other German Makes

Germany has had, and still has, several custom truck builders but, as in other countries, few general purpose truck makers have succeeded in the past twenty years against competition from the giant firms. Kaelble and Faun now make trucks for the construction industry but not general haulage models. Krupp was forced to stop making trucks following Government intervention as a result of its wartime armaments contracts, and Büssing and Hanomag-Henschel were taken over by MAN and Mercedes-Benz respectively, while Borgward went out of business at the start of the sixties.

Krupp was forced to discontinue its road haulage range in 1968 as part of a war reparation agreement after which its transport side made only truck-mounted cranes. Atkinson planned to use the former Krupp cab on its 1969 export range but few were produced. Krupp used its own 2-stroke diesels until, in 1963, it began to build Cummins engines under licence. This 1967 KF380 outfit for 38 tonnes gtw has a Krupp-Cummins 275bhp V-8 diesel.

Büssing, famous for its underfloor engined trucks, has belonged to MAN since 1971. Its name had all but disappeared by the late seventies but was revived for a new underfloor engined range with MAN cab and other components. Shown here is a 1964 Commodore SK front engined tractive unit with 192bhp 11.4-litre 6-cylinder Büssing diesel. A forward control version was also available.

Kaelble has made heavy haulage tractors throughout the sixties and seventies and here is one from 1960 used for transferring laden railway trucks from customer's depots by road to the rail sidings. It is a 4 × 2 tractor with 230bhp Kaelble 6-cylinder diesel engine.

Hanomag and Henschel merged in the late sixties and for a time made vehicles bearing both names, the former having previously specialized in small and the latter in medium and large trucks. Hanomag owned Tempo and much of the former Borgward factory, which became the home of Mercedes-Benz derived Hanomag-Henschel light trucks after the Mercedes-Benz takeover in the early seventies. The illustration shows a 2½-ton capacity 4 × 4 Hanomag truck of the mid sixties. This example has a 2.8-litre petrol or diesel 4-cylinder engine of 50 or 70bhp.

A 38-tonne gtw Henschel F221 at work in 1968 with a large transit concrete mixer. This model had a 235bhp 6-cylinder diesel. Henschel had just joined forces with Hanomag at this stage, before which their output had been as low as 3,500 per annum.

A new make of truck in 1963 from a long-established farm tractor maker was the Eicher Transexpress. This is a 1966 example with 4-cylinder, air-cooled 3.9-litre, 68bhp Eicher diesel and 4- or 5-speed gearbox. Load capacity was around 3000kg. In 1970 Massey-Ferguson bought a 30 per cent stake in Eicher and thereafter it concentrated on farm tractors once more.

By the time that Borgward went into liquidation in 1961 it was making forward and normal control models of up to 6 tonnes capacity. The largest was based on the Hansa-Lloyd, whose original factory at Bremen Carl Borgward had taken over in 1929 (although he had not called the trucks by his own name until after the war). The example shown is a 1960 B655 with 6-cylinder, 5-litre 110bhp Borgward diesel and a payload of up to 5,600kg. Much of Borgward's factory was later acquired by Hanomag.

In the early sixties Faun made normal road haulage models (usually with Ford engines) for loads as small as 1500kg, but by the mid seventies its only general trucks were heavy models and it was concentrating on special purpose vehicles like municipal trucks, earthmovers and heavy tractors. This is a 300bhp tractor with Deutz air-cooled engine. It had 6-wheel drive and could haul trailers with a gtw in excess of 130 tons.

ITALY

The number of firms making trucks in Italy has fallen dramatically during the past two decades with Fiat gaining a virtual monopoly. In the sixties Lancia, Alfa-Romeo and Fiat's OM division all offered wide ranges, and specialist heavy vehicles were made by OMT (AEC engines in 1964), SAME (of farm tractor fame who made trucks for only a short time from 1963), Viberti, Perlini and Astra. Whilst the last three still make small numbers of off-road vehicles and have been joined in the specialist trade by Man Meccanica and the new firm Sirmac, Fiat has cornered the market for normal goods vehicles and is also a partner with Klöckner-Humboldt-Deutz in IVECO (founded in 1974) which controls Magirus-Deutz, OM, Lancia and Unic.

A current Fiat model new in 1976 is the 190NT33 for 40-tonnes gcw. It has a 330bhp V-8 diesel and 8 or 13 forward gears. It is also available as a longer wheelbase 19-tonne gvw rigid.

With a payload of 7.5 tonnes plus trailer this Fiat 643N of 1967 had a 161bhp 6-cylinder diesel and 2-range 5-speed gearbox. For tough, no frills operation this cab style was retained well into the seventies alongside the new generation models.

Right   OM has been a Fiat subsidiary since 1938 but until the seventies it was very much a separate marque, accounting for 17.41 per cent of goods vehicle sales in Italy in 1966 (which included little vans and pickups) against Fiat's 67.81 per cent. In the seventies OMs became almost indistinguishable from Fiats. This is an OM120C in 1968 with 7410cc, 154bhp diesel engine and 8-tonne payload capacity. Lighter models have been supplied by OM to Saurer to complement the Swiss firm's range throughout the period.

As part of IVECO, Lancia has made only special purpose and military commercial vehicles since the mid seventies. However, in the sixties it made a fairly full range of trucks, which, however seldom, accounted for more than 1 per cent of the Italian market. This is their Esagamma E of 1967 with 10.5-litre 209bhp 6-cylinder diesel engine.

SCANDINAVIA AND THE NETHERLANDS

Sweden dominates the commercial vehicle industry in this area with Scania and Volvo. The growth of the Swedish industry during the period has been phenomenal, and from being almost unheard of in 1960 it now supplies a high proportion of Europe's heavy vehicle needs. Scania and Volvo also have a large market share in South America, supplied by factories in Peru (Volvo) and Brazil (Scania). Whilst Scania concentrates on maximum legal capacity vehicles, Volvo's range includes medium trucks as well, and since the early seventies it has been associated with Magirus-Deutz, Saviem and DAF in the 'Club of Four'. Scania has had technical links with Mack since the forties and Volvo has collaborated with Mack on gas turbine development since 1973. In 1978 the Norwegian government attempted to buy a 40 per cent stake in Volvo but was unsuccessful.

Finland produces the SISU, and in the sixties produced the Vanaja as well. The Finnish industry has close links with Britain, AEC having supplied the former Vanaja with engines, and Leyland and Rolls-Royce supplying SISU, a firm which is 10 per cent owned by both Scania and Leyland.

In the Netherlands there is DAF, which until the late sixties used a high proportion of British components, including Leyland engines, and since 1972 has been a third owned by the American International Harvester Co. Also in the Netherlands are the specialized on-off-road vehicle makers, RAM, Terberg, Ginaf and FTF. The latter, like DAF, started as a trailer maker, while the others grew from military vehicle reconditioning.

Alfa-Romeo was another firm to make medium weight trucks in the sixties, though since then it has concentrated on light vehicles based on Saviem designs. This is their 1963 Mille with 11-litre 174bhp 6-cylinder diesel engine. It was for 16 tons gvw. The Mille was also offered as a trailing axle 6-wheeler, and was available from 1958 to 1964.

During the sixties Scania was known by its full title of Scania-Vabis but in 1968/9 the Vabis portion was discontinued (the two firms had merged in 1911). Here we see a 1967 example of the 76 range, which had first appeared in 1963. It had a 275bhp 6-cylinder diesel and was intended for 38 tons gtw.

The Volvo Titan was the first normal production turbocharged truck in 1954 and this is an example in the early sixties with 9.6-litre 217bhp turbocharged diesel engine and 5-speed gearbox.

Although the forward control 110 Series introduced in 1968 is now the best known high-powered, heavy Scania outside Sweden, normal control models are still popular in its homeland. Shown is a fibreglass-bonnetted 140 using the 14-litre V-8 250bhp engine introduced in 1969 and now available with outputs of up to 375bhp.

The forward control L420 of 1963. It was for 2½- to 3-tonnes and had a V-8, 3½-litre 114bhp petrol engine. Volvo had introduced their first 'Tiptop' tilt cab in 1962 and this later became widely known on the F84/86 range.

One of several manufacturers to use AEC engines before the Leyland takeover was Vanajan Autotehdas Oy and here we see a 1960 Vanaja with AV690 154bhp 6-cylinder 11.3-litre diesel engine on trial in arctic conditions.

The 80 Series of Volvo trucks first appeared in 1965 and this is a 1967 F88 with 260bhp turbocharged diesel designed for gtw of up to 70 tonnes. The F88 and 89 were replaced by the new F10 and F12 in 1977.

A DAF AT1900 DS 6 × 4 tipper of 1964, with the cab that, with styling modifications, had been used since the early days of the company as a truck maker in the late forties. This example had a DAF 165bhp 6-cylinder turbocharged diesel engine.

Ginaf made vehicles from ex 1939—45 military truck components and as these ran out it used a proportion of modern parts. Here we see a 6 × 6 FS200 example of around 1970 with DAF 226bhp diesel engine. Current models use DAF cabs as well.

Floor had previously built trailers and marketed Mack vehicles in Holland, but in 1966 they unveiled this FTF truck with Detroit 238bhp V-6 diesel and Allison 6-speed automatic transmission. Current models employ British Motor Panels cabs in place of the stark Floor-made example shown here.

As this shape of DAF is still around in 1979, it is hard to believe that its advanced styling first appeared some fifteen years earlier. This is a 1966 TT 2600 DP 38-tonne gtw outfit with 226bhp diesel engine.

Right Normal control SISUs acquired this revised fibreglass bonnet styling in the mid sixties and here we see a 1968 6 × 4 model with Rolls-Royce Eagle 260bhp diesel working at 30 tons gcw.

Terberg had built modified US Army trucks with Mercedes cabs until this SF1400-437 was made in 1970. It had a Mercedes-Benz 185bhp 6-cylinder diesel engine and 5-speed synchromesh gearbox. Current heavy models employ Volvo engines and cabs

Whilst AEC was supplying engines to Vanaja, their competitor Leyland was exporting 126bhp 6-cylinder diesels to SISU for various models including this K-26 tipper chassis. Dating from 1961 it had 4 x 4 and a gvw of 13.8 tons. A 5-speed gearbox with 2-speed transfer box was fitted.

FRANCE

France had almost as many makers of medium and heavy trucks as Britain at the start of the sixties but in the past twenty years these have been severely reduced by takeovers and competition from other countries.

Many of the best known makes have changed hands many times, and, as in Britain with Leyland, several have come under State ownership, or else been acquired by foreign manufacturers. France retains strong trading ties with many of its former colonies, and these take the bulk of her truck exports, though China has also been a useful customer. Berliet is the largest of the heavy makers, accounting for 50 per cent of the over 6-ton market in 1972 with Saviem second (30 per cent) and Unic third (19 per cent).

Berliet

Berliet has had a somewhat chequered career during the past twenty years. Despite being the largest heavy vehicle maker in France with a production potential of 150 chassis per day it has suffered a number of financial problems and after rescue by Citroën in 1967 it passed to the state-controlled Renault concern in 1975, where it joined the same stable as Saviem. It has made special purpose and off-road heavy vehicles during the period as well as an advanced

This highly advanced Stradair 10 of 1965 had air suspension and tilt cab with room for three people abreast. Payload was 5000kg and the engine was Berliet's 4-cylinder 3.86-litre diesel of 80bhp output coupled to a 5-speed gearbox (synchromesh on the top 4 ratios). The Airlam suspension consisted of torque rods and 6 air cushions, 4 of which were on the rear axle. This model and its 120bhp 6-cylinder sister was later revised as a Citroën-Berliet and by 1972 had lost its protruding snout and air suspension.

range of normal road haulage models, and is France's largest exporter of trucks over 6 tons, selling over 40 per cent of its production overseas, especially in Africa, where it has a large assembly plant in Algeria. (Its Moroccan plant is now locally controlled and ironically makes Berliets with Leyland engines and axles.)

Citroën's new medium truck range in 1965 included the 350, 600 and 700 models, carrying 3.5, 6 and 7 tonnes respectively. This is the 350 with choice of Perkins or MAN diesels and Citroën petrol engines.

In 1972 Berliet introduced a new range of heavy tractive units and rigids for 38 tons gvw with new high torque 'Maxi Couple' V-8 engines of 320bhp output. Here, one with tyre chains fights winter conditions in the Alps at the head of a convoy of Volvos and Mercedes.

Citroën

Before their takeover of Berliet in 1967, Citroën made trucks of up to about 3 tons capacity and from 1955 they also had a financial interest in (and eventually controlled) Panhard, who made heavier commercial vehicles. In 1974 the Citroën-Berliet group hit financial difficulties, with the result that Citroën joined Peugeot and Berliet joined Renault. Peugeot-Citroën have only made light trucks, but with their takeover of Chrysler in Europe in 1978 they have acquired the Spanish Dodge/Barreiros and British Dodge/Karrier factories.

Saviem

Saviem, whose initials stand for Industrial Vehicles and Mechanical Equipment in French, was formed in 1955 when Renault took over Somua and Latil. The Isobloc and Chausson PSV factories were added in 1956 and 1958. The various original manufacturers were phased out by 1960, their individual names being remembered on trucks by the initials SAVIEM LRS.

Saviem developed close technical ties with MAN in the sixties and nowadays uses many common parts, including engines and cabs. Its light trucks are sold by Alfa Romeo in Italy and it has jointly developed medium trucks with DAF, Magirus-Deutz and Volvo from 1971 (Club of Four). Since 1975 Berliet has been owned by Saviem-Renault.

Right Saviem's 3-ton gvw to 35-ton gtw range in the mid sixties. On the top is a 70bhp Super Goelette, then a 126bhp S7, a 150bhp JL29 and then a 235bhp JM240. All these were designed from the outset as Saviems though the cab styling of the JM derives from the former forward control Latil, whilst the smaller models have some Renault affinities.

Showing its MAN connections is this 1974 SM21 180 with steel tilt cab and 7.258-litre 180bhp diesel. It is for 21 tons gtw.

Unic

Unic had been a subsidiary of Simca since 1951 and for a time trucks based on the old Ford-derived Simca (Simca had taken over Ford's French interests in 1954) were made as well as traditional Unics and Saurers (whose French factory had become part of the group in 1956). To add to the complexities the light to medium weight bonnetted range used sheet metal bought from Fiat and almost identical to some of their models.

Chrysler bought an interest in Simca in 1958 and gained control in 1963, then in 1966 Fiat set up a French truck branch, which acquired Unic from Chrysler. Since the formation of IVECO by KHD and Fiat in 1975 Unics have become known as Unic-Fiat.

Three styles of cab in use by Unic in 1963. The two forward control models are derived from the old Simca Cargo whilst the smaller of the bonnetted models uses sheet metal designed by Fiat. The archetypal heavy Unic for up to 29.3 tonnes gtw (second from left) was also available with Saurer name badge in the late fifties.

Reviving a famous name from its old normal control range is this 1972 Unic Izoard T340A 38-tonne tractive unit (a model introduced in 1971) with 340bhp V-8 diesel and Fiat cab.

When Willème sold Austin-Morris trucks in the early sixties they bore Willème-BMC badges. This is their G150 model for 7.5-tonne loads. It had the BMC 5.7-litre 118bhp diesel.

Willème

Willème specialized in heavy duty, special purpose vehicles and in 1962 became associated with AEC, whose engines they used in their own vehicles and whose British models they marketed in France (at the lighter end of the market they also sold BMC trucks). They were later acquired by Perez and Raimond, who held the French concession for GM Detroit diesels. In the early seventies the revived firm began to offer heavy haulage and custom built trucks once more.

Although normal road haulage models were revived in 1972, it was with heavy tractors and off-road vehicles that Willème re-established their name. This is a 1976 TG150 tractor for gtw of up to 180,000kg. A 400bhp V-12 Detroit diesel was standard, but Mercedes, Caterpillar or Cummins engines could be specified. It had a 13-speed Fuller gearbox and a tilt cab.

Left A 35-tonne gtw articulated outfit with Willème's own 6-cylinder 190bhp diesel and 6-speed gearbox. It dates from shortly before the AEC involvement in 1962.

Other French Makes

There have been several small firms making commercial vehicles of one sort or another, notably in the early sixties. The old Laffly firm just staggered into the period, while Bernard had a temporary new lease of life under Mack control. Labourier made a few special-purpose off-road trucks and crane carriers, whilst a new make of tipper was the Perkins-engined ALM in the mid sixties which bore a close resemblance to the modernized Second World War military trucks that were such a part of the Dutch market. FAR have made mechanical horses throughout the period, originally based on the Scammell Scarab, and Sovam, best known for their Peugeot-based mobile shops, also made front-wheel drive Perkins 6.354 engined trucks in the late sixties.

The old established Bernard concern joined forces with Mack in 1963 and this was the first result, a Mack 211bhp-engined 35-ton gtw tractive unit. The liaison was not fruitful and in 1966 Mack withdrew and Bernard abandoned trucks, becoming a maker of diesel engines and components within the Renault group.

SPAIN

The Spanish truck industry has grown in importance over the last twenty years and now exports trucks in considerable quantities. In the fifties it had Pegaso (who had technical links with Leyland) and Barreiros heavy vehicles, but practically everything lighter (apart from Nazar) was of foreign origin though often assembled in Spain; these included Alfa-Romeo, Ford/Ebro, Austin/SAVA (merged with Pegaso in 1966), Land-Rover/Santana, DKW and Citroën. At the start of the period AEC had close ties with Barreiros but in the late sixties the Chrysler Corporation moved in and in 1978 substituted the name Dodge on all former Barreiros truck models (many had been marketed overseas before that as Dodges). Shortly afterwards Chrysler's Spanish and other European interests were acquired by Peugeot-Citroën. From producing Fords under licence Ebro developed its own trucks in the sixties and in 1971 acquired the makers of Siata light and Avia medium weight trucks (it also makes Jeeps under licence).

A typical Barreiros of the late sixties using cab pressings that carried on for the next ten years. This example is for 42-ton gtw and has a 12-litre 6-cylinder 285bhp diesel engine.

Left The famous old armaments firm of Hotchkiss had made light and medium trucks since the late thirties and in 1954 had joined forces with the Delahaye car and truck firm. Hotchkiss made Jeeps under licence in the fifties and sixties and was French distributor for Leyland, Albion and Scammell. It also made its own medium weight trucks in small numbers until the seventies. An all-wheel drive Hotchkiss PL 70/80 model of 1968 is shown, with 4-cylinder 3456cc petrol engine developing 134bhp and 4-speed gearbox with 2-speed transfer box. It had a tilt cab and was suitable for loads plus body work from 3680–4415kg dependent on specification.

Avia have used this cab shape from 1968 to the present time and this is an early example on their 6500 chassis. It had a Perkins 100bhp 6-cylinder diesel (Perkins have had a major share in the firm since 1966) and was for loads of up to 6.9 tonnes.

Right A 1973 Pegaso 2082 model with 352bhp diesel, 9-speed Fuller gearbox and tilt cab. Though its legal gvw in Spain was 38 tonnes it could handle far higher weights as a heavy haulage tractor. Pegaso models of under 6 tons capacity are produced by their associates SAVA.

From 1941 Ebro made trucks based on Ford components and this continued until the mid fifties, after which local content steadily increased. This is a model C-150 for 1,500kg loads, made in 1967 and still showing signs of its Ford ancestry.

Ebro moved into the heavy market with their tilt-cab P range of 1976. These can have Perkins 129, 137 or 173bhp, 6-cylinder and V-8 diesels and are for payloads of up to 13.5 tonnes on 2 axles and 19.1 tonnes on 3 axles.

Pegaso's distinctive style of the sixties and early seventies, shown by a 1968 2011-A model. It had a newly introduced supercharged 10.5-litre diesel which developed 260bhp and was for 38-tonne gtw. At that time Pegaso were producing almost 10,000 heavy trucks and bus/coaches per year.

Much smaller than Saurer/Berna is Moway, which nowadays makes only special-purpose vehicles, and FBW, which custom builds trucks for municipal and road haulage purposes. Other Swiss commercial vehicles tend to be light 4 × 4s for use in the mountainous districts and are outside our scope, though Meili now makes examples up to 7 tons gvw.

SWITZERLAND

Saurer and Berna have been linked throughout the period and their products have been identical for many years, though they retain their individual names to aid marketing strategy in French and German speaking districts of Switzerland. Saurer had factories in France until the late fifties and in Austria until the sixties and has had close links with OM since the twenties and today markets the lighter OMs with its own nameplates in Switzerland.

A Berna 4VF (4DF if lettered Saurer) of 1975 with front-mounted 6-cylinder 200bhp diesel and 6-forward-speed gearbox. Throughout the period Saurer/Berna have also made normal control versions with 2- or 4-wheel drive.

This underfloor engined Saurer 5DU dates from 1963 and was for 8.5-tonne loads. it had a 6-cylinder diesel of either 160 or 210bhp output and, with the engine out of the way, there was room for four abreast seating in the low-mounted cab.

This attractive cab style of 1968 is still used today by FBW on its forward control models. The example shown was for 6-tonne loads and had a 130bhp, 6-cylinder, underfloor-mounted, diesel engine and 8-speed synchro-mesh gearbox. The steel and aluminium cab was constructed by Ramseier and Jenzer of Berne

Mowag made this MD-4F/LW truck in 1963 but became increasingly specialized over the next ten years, concentrating on military and off-road vehicles, for which it made its own multi-fuel engines. When the example shown was made the firm used principally Chrysler and Büssing engines and this 4-tonner has a Chrysler V-8 petrol engine developing 202bhp, which made a 4-speed gearbox adequate for the load, even in mountainous Switzerland.

This advanced cab styling appeared on the Steyr 890, 990 and 1290 range in 1969 and it still current today. Shown is a 1974 1290 model, designed specially for drawbar trailer work. As a rigid, it could carry 12 tons and had a 350bhp V-8 supercharged 12-litre diesel and 8-speed gearbox plus crawler and reverse. Annual Steyr production in 1978 was 6,000 commercial vehicles.

AUSTRIA

Austria has had a long history of producing foreign vehicles under licence or of importing manufacturing technology. In the seventies it has developed close ties with the German motor industry; Steyr with Mercedes-Benz, and ÖAF and its bus making associate Gräf & Stift (which made trucks through the sixties) with MAN. Until the early years of our period, Saurer vehicles of Swiss origin were also made in Austria.

Having made Fiats under licence for many years, Austro-Fiat changed its name after the Second World War to ÖAF and developed its own vehicles (at which point Steyr assembled Fiat trucks for a time). In 1963, when this 9¼-tonne capacity Tornado 9-200 was made, the firm was using its own 180bhp 6-cylinder diesels or alternatively Cummins 202bhp V-8s or Leyland 200bhp 6-cylinder diesels. A forward control version was offered and 6- or 12-speed gearboxes were available.

Left Although this Steyr 586Z dates from 1966 its appearance had remained largely unchanged since the 1950s (until the early sixties it had freestanding headlights). It was for 7- to 8-tonne loads and had a 6-cylinder Steyr 132bhp diesel and 5-forward-speed constant-mesh gearbox.

An ÖAF FTL 9-215M 9-tonner of 1972 with Leyland 0.680 6-cylinder diesel engine. This was to be the firm's last wholly local design, as by 1975 MAN cabs, engines and other components had spread across much of their range.

Although sharing the same cab (with different grille) as the contemporary ÖAF, this 1964 Gräf & Stift KF-160/38 tipper for 9-tonne loads used its own 160bhp 6-cylinder diesel with the option of a 200bhp 6-cylinder Mercedes-Benz diesel.

OTHER COUNTRIES

In other sections we have looked at the principal truck manufacturing countries; now we consider the makes from elsewhere. Most semi-industrialized nations have some form of truck assembly operation either making their own indigenous brands using imported major components or else making well known trucks imported as ckd (completely knocked down) kits of parts. In the former category comes the Irish Dennison, Australian Leader and International ACCO, Canadian Scot, Mexican Ramirez and the South African Ralph and in the latter the Indian Hindustan and Ashok Leyland and Turkish Morris and GM based Genoto. Even ckd makes are increasing their local component content to the point when often only engines and transmissions have to be imported.

Canada had its own indigenous industry making special trucks for the lumber trade but one by one these were all acquired by American manufacturers during the past twenty years. Hayes survived under Mack ownership until 1975 when Peterbilt bought the concern, only to close it down in the following year. However, the International-owned Pacific continues to prosper alongside Scot. Sicard made its own trucks into the seventies, but its plants now make models of Dart, Kenworth and Peterbilt.

It is many years since the smaller European countries like Denmark and Belgium were able to support their own industries, and they now rely on locally produced foreign makes with the exception of MOL, who make custom built trucks in Belgium, primarily for export. Prior to that Belgium had the old-established Miesse firm, which was still making trucks in 1967 with Detroit diesel engines.

As more and more heavy trucks are made from proprietary components it seems likely that many other countries will soon be able to buy in parts to found or re-establish their own truck manufacturing businesses. However such countries as China continue to rely on their own resources, and as a result make extremely basic vehicles, which no doubt perform adequately, but are many years behind their Western counterparts.

Typical of the trucks produced for Canada's lumber industry by Hayes, Canadian Kenworth, Scot and Pacific, is this Hayes HD400 of the early seventies. It was available with various proprietary components and engines of American origin until 1976, when Hayes' owners, Mack Trucks, suspended Hayes production.

MOL is a Belgian trailer making firm which in the mid sixties added special purpose trucks to its range. This is a 1965 MK455/25 all-wheel-drive tipper chassis for 25 tonnes gvw. It shows a mixture of Magirus-Deutz and American military vehicle influence.

Typical of the way in which some local assembly plants for foreign makes evolve their own designs is this Turkish Morris TM140 of 1970. Vehicles of similar appearance are still made today and it is interesting to note the combination of Austin, Morris and Leyland badges on the radiator. A 5.6-litre 120bhp 6-cylinder diesel drove through a 5-forward-speed gearbox in this 11,000kg gvw model.

This is a 1976 MOL 6 × 6 model HFT 2666 concrete mixer chassis for 26,000kg gvw. It has a Deutz V-6 185bhp air-cooled diesel engine and 5-speed gearbox plus 2-speed transfer box.

Right Many small local makes have been developed by established trailer makers, and this is the current Ramirez R-20 from Trailers de Monterrey in Mexico. It uses a locally built Cummins 230bhp diesel and American-origin transmission components. Most trucks used in South America are either imported from North America or else locally assembled Mercedes-Benz, SISU and other European and American makes. Mexico also has Dina trucks, partly owned by International, and had several other brands during the period.

The Scot from Canada is another assembled truck using a variety of North American proprietary components and Cummins or Detroit diesels. Shown is a 1978 6 × 4 model available with engines of up to 450bhp and up to 15 forward gears. The bonnet tilts forward for access and is made of fibreglass, and the cab and styling are by Scot, who until 1976 used Ford Louisville cabs on their conventional models.

This late sixties Jay Fong DD340 from mainland China resembled American trucks of thirty years before. It had a capacity of 3.5 tonnes, which was nearly a ton less than its unladen weight. It had a petrol engine of undisclosed output and was intended for tough basic transport with minimal maintenance.

The first Australian built RFW (the initials of its designer Bob Whitehead) appeared in 1969 and, as can be seen, it used a Bedford KM cab. Detroit, Perkins, Cummins, Deutz, AEC, Caterpillar and Scania engines were available, and a 200bhp example of the latter make was fitted in the initial truck shown. The RFW competed against imports and such locally assembled foreign trucks as Foden, ERF, Oshkosh and International as well as the mid-seventies newcomer, the Leader.

The International ACCO-A series of trucks was developed especially for Australian manufacture and operating conditions, and was the result of an 11.5 million dollar investment. Perkins, International and Cummins diesels (or International gas engines) are used of 131 to 320bhp. This tilt-cab tipper is for 42,000lbs gvw and versions can have 5-, 10- or 13-speed manual gearboxes or 5-speed automatics.

Ireland's first heavy truck manufacturer is Dennison, who made vehicles in small quantities from August 1977. Shown is a Rolls-Royce 265bhp engined 30-ton gvw tipper with Motor Panels tilt cab and Fuller 9-speed gearbox.

Since 1966 Australian built Atkinsons have borne little resemblance to their UK counterparts. This example of 1966 has the steel-framed fibreglass cab produced for Atkinson Vehicles (Australia) Pty Ltd. by Reinforced Plastics Pty Ltd. and it is shown here with sleeper attachment. Engines of British or American origin are used for Australian Atkinsons, this unit having a 150bhp Gardner diesel. International acquired Atkinson's Australian organization when it bought Seddon-Atkinson, but the Australian Atkinson retains its identity.

INDEX OF TRUCK MAKERS